The Ambitious Capitalist's Guide to Investing in GOLD

How to invest in GOLD without Getting Your Fingers Burned!

By Mike Bradley

Table of Contents

Introduction

Gold is certainly not the rarest metal to be found but nevertheless the total volume of gold ever smelted would still only form a 20 metre cube, although it is estimated that the Earth's seas and oceans contain nearly 20 million tonnes of gold with even more within the Earth's molten core... and of all the 92 naturally occurring elements to be found on Earth, gold is only the 58th most common... but as far as rare metals are concerned, it is right up there! In order of rarity, the most rare metals to be found on Earth are (in order): Iridium, Rhodium, Rhenium, Gold, Palladium, Platinum, and Silver. The only remarkable thing is that Platinum is more common than gold although much more pricey. That is because of the difficulty in extracting Platinum as 80% is still buried under the ground in South Africa.

Gold has fascinated man for many thousands of years and even now in many quarters it is the ultimate expression of wealth as it continues to be mined in ever increasing volumes with the main producer currently being China. Although, having said that, about 50% of the gold ever mined has come from a single place in South Africa called Witwatersrand.

Many governments still use gold in order to give their paper currency value and because of that, one might suspect that either China, Russia or the United States holds the largest volume of gold. In fact, 11% of all the gold in the world is owned by Indian households and India continues to be the biggest consumer of gold!

Indian housewives have more gold than the combined reserves of the IMF, the USA and several other countries!

As far as gold as a future resource is concerned, it is believed that only about 20% of the gold which can be mined from underground has been found. The other 80% is still available!

Chapter 1 – All about Gold

A History of Gold Investment

It is believed that it was the Egyptians who were the first to smelt gold. Most of us have seen photographs of Tutankhamen's sarcophagus. That was made from approximately 100 kg of gold. The Egyptians also used gold for coinage as well as ornaments and jewellery. It is the ancient Egyptians who first treated gold as a valuable commodity, obviously without realising its comparative rarity.

The ancient Persians were also great users of gold and it was Alexander the Great of Greece who plundered their treasures, including tons of gold and so introduced Greece to the value of gold.

The next development was with the Roman Empire and its monetary system. The Romans liked the portability of gold bullion and gold coin and used it extensively throughout, spreading their wealth from Rome towards the four corners of their empire.

By the time Alexander the Great was fighting the Persians and plundering their gold, the Chinese already had gold *coins* which they called Ying Yuan... and interestingly, the Yuan is still the unit of basic currency in China.

We all know about the 16th century Spanish conquistadors and their quests for Astec and Inca gold, which had both been discovered independently and also turned into all sorts of artefacts similar to the ones found in ancient Egypt. For a while, the requisition of gold from South America and its transportation to Europe became one of Spain's major industries – to the joy of the British Navy which made its own living from stealing it from the Spanish!

Gradually, pure gold coins went out of use although they continued to be traded between the very rich – until the 19th century when a universal gold standard was introduced. Until the beginning of the First World War, the Industrial Revolution and the massive acceleration in worldwide trade was as a direct result of a rapidly evolving and stable financial system, based on individual states ownership of gold.

For the 80 or 90 years following the end of the First World War, gold certainly appreciated in value but I think at quite a steady rate while the world states gradually increased their gold holdings which provided the backbone for the steady increase in global trade.
The financial crises which began soon after the turn of the millennium, and which culminated in the banking crisis followed by bank bailouts and then the so-called quantitative easing, or printing of money saw investors looking to gold as a stable investment rather than the gradual devaluation of money through the continued money printing encouraged by governments and executed by central banks.

Once again, gold is a fashionable and potentially very profitable investment, especially as there are once again rumours of yet another imminent financial crash, primarily as a result of overinflated equity prices the use of quantitative easing as an attempt to boost ailing economies all over the world.

When we talk about modern investment in gold we are not necessarily talking about its ornamental use any more. The electronics industry for instance, is only one of the uses of high-tech gold. It is interesting to know that even the space shuttles contained approximately 40 kg of gold... and continuing with the high tech theme, more gold is recovered from a ton of old personal computers than from about 20 tonnes of gold ore – *that* is how essential its physical properties have become to new technology, primarily within the electronics industry.

Although gold is very abundant on paper – it is highly unlikely that it's going to be extracted from the Earth's molten core, or even from the world's oceans so it is definitely considered a very finite resource but one with increasingly diverse uses.

It continues to be the primary investment in an economically uncertain world because unlike paper money, it has a real intrinsic value.

Even if you are a seasoned investor, or should I say *especially* if you are a seasoned and knowledgeable investor, I bet that quite a large percentage of your portfolio is invested in some form of gold or maybe another precious metal.

Facts about Gold

One of the great ancient attractions of gold was the fact that it has its own unique colour. Most other metals are of various shades of grey. The fact that it does not oxidise in air and maintains its shine for ever is what initially seduced humans to treat it with such veneration.

It is one of the softest metals, and in order to give it any sort of tensile strength, impurities or other metals have to be added to it. They say that a very pure piece of gold can be moulded with the fingers – that is how malleable it can be. Just to put its malleability into perspective, a single ounce of gold can be rolled or beaten into a 300 ft.² sheet and can be rolled thinly enough to be transparent!

It is also extremely ductile. As an example that same ounce of gold can be pulled or stretched into a thread about 5 miles long – hence it's continued use in high-end embroidery!

Obviously the above qualities and properties refer to what is known as 24 carat, or pure gold. As the carat of gold decreases, so the purity of the gold decreases. Even 18 carat gold is only 75% pure – with silver having been added, although other metals are also added occasionally, among them copper, platinum and even iron in order to either change properties or colour.

In jewellery, many people find the word carat confusing because they assume that as it refers to a specific weight when applied to say diamonds, the same applies to gold. In fact a diamond carat is

200 mg whereas a *gold carat* is totally unrelated to weight and simply expresses the purity of the gold and indicates the percentage of gold present.

For instance a 22 carat gold ring contains (22/24)% gold, which is 91.6%... this assumes that 24 carat is pure gold... so that 9 carat ring you bought your fiancé is only 9/24% or 37.5% gold. So do beware in future when buying gold because I have known people to buy 9 carat gold at 24 carat gold prices!

Here's another very simple statistic which perhaps expresses the comparative scarcity of gold and that is that the amount of gold which has been dug up and smelted since the beginning of time is still less than the amount of steel currently created throughout the world.

Although China is currently the world's major gold producer, it is closely followed by both Russia and America as well as Australia. South Africa which used to be the world's major gold miner is now in fourth or fifth place.

Those of you who have either drunk Goldwasser with its flecks of gold leaf or eaten high-end food which has been covered in gold leaf will know that gold is non-toxic and in fact we all have a small amount of it within our bloodstream.

Gold Supply and Demand

We have established that gold has a certain rarity but it has the right balance of volume and appeal which does make it so popular as an investment.

The Earth hasn't always had a gold supply and although it is a known phenomenon that earthquakes can turn water into gold, almost all of the Earth's gold arrived in a shower of meteorites which hit the Earth about 200 million years after the earth's formation... and it is found on every single continent.

Gold has now entered every part of our lives. Its appeal is not purely to do with wealth or the acquisition of assets because in the last 5000 years it has also developed a great cultural appeal – for instance in the self-adornment industry. Yes it does have a significant role in investment and especially nowadays in its role as a tool to mitigate against risk in the natural portfolios. It also is a device for maintaining and protecting the wealth of entire nations and of course nowadays we all carry a small amount of gold around with us all the time in our smart phones.

Its importance to our lives cannot be overestimated and currently demand is outstripping production for the very first time with countries such as China, India and Turkey between them having created a demand which takes up nearly 50% of the world's annual production. In China's case, it is a matter of technology and commerce as well as jewellery, whereas India and Turkey see gold as an investment, primarily in the jewellery industry.

These markets can do nothing else but grow over the next few years, for no other reason than their populations are growing at an accelerated rate with both the Indian and Chinese economies projected to experience economic growth in double figures. Gold is certainly becoming a feature of their future wealth not only because of their numbers but because of the aspirational nature of their new rich.

Culturally, they see gold as an investment which cannot only be traded but can be handed down through the family to future generations.

Although jewellery is a surprising major player in the gold markets, the investment industry also takes advantage of gold's ability by using it to protect against downside risks when part of an investment portfolio. This has certainly been the case and has increased demand within the last 10 years during times of financial chaos. It is recognised as an excellent way of protecting capital.

Investment in gold *accounts* represents as much as 30% of the total global demand for the metal. Both Exchange Traded Funds as well as investment in the metal itself in the form of bullion and coin... we shall be covering specifics in a later section.

There are those who wonder whether central banks have any gold left, especially as production is lagging behind demand but it is fair to say that central banks attitudes towards gold have changed substantially since the financial crisis of 2007/8. In the last few years, central banks have been net buyers of gold and now representing about 15% of total world demand. Why are they suddenly so keen on investing in gold? Exactly for the same reason that investment managers are, that is to say in order to mitigate against other losses – basically to help them with their risk management.

Unlike many other investments, it is now well established that in the long term gold is always able to maintain its purchasing power. The other reason central banks as well as investment managers like gold is the fact that there will always be a market for gold whether they are buying or selling. It is the liquidity of the market which makes it such an attractive mid-to long-term asset.

The remainder of the world's demand for gold (and one suspects it is going to be a continuously growing demand) is in the field of technology, through all sorts of applications where gold's electrical and physical characteristics are so useful. As the best conductor of heat and electricity coupled with its resistance to corrosion it looks as if it's going to stay in demand by the technology industry for as long as there is a technology industry which relies on the flow of electrons from A to B!

Although the space industry has slowed in the last 20 years, gold is still very much in demand within fuel cells as well as electronics. The automotive industry has discovered its catalytic properties which are being used more and more in favour of Platinum.

One of the newer industries is found in the field of nanotechnology where once again gold's physical and electrical properties are making it possible for this field to accelerate.

So, there are four main areas which create the rapidly accelerating demand for gold. The jewellery industry, investment, banking and the new and emerging technologies.

One could argue that the first three overlap each other to a certain extent and we are going to be looking very specifically at the type of gold investment which is available to a private individual.

Chapter 2 – Solid Gold

Gold Coins & Small Bars

The $1 million coin from Australia weighs 1000 kg, is made from 99.90% pure gold and is currently worth about $45 million. Although the coin is legal tender, it is not the sort of amount we're going to be discussing. We'll stick to smaller denominations of both coin and bullion. Although, as a matter of interest, the world's largest gold bar weighs 250 kg!

The opportunities for investing in solid gold had never been greater because nowadays it is possible for the man in the street not only to buy gold jewellery but also to invest in bullion and coin.

You no longer have to disappear to the Yukon or Siberia in order to find gold. Nowadays, you can even buy it on eBay, Amazon or any number of online traders – and you can start your collection or investment with the bar as small as 1 gram!

If you are not a jewellery hoarder, the most common way of investing in gold is via the bullion gold bar or the coin.

Although some countries (for instance Lichtenstein) will sell you gold at the counter and Switzerland's banks will sell you gold bullion, most others will have to deal through middlemen. I only mention that because each stage of the purchase chain is an added expense although for most of us, the bullion dealer is a necessary evil.

Before we go into specifics let's have another definition so that we understand what we are buying. Whenever you see the word bullion, it refers to gold which is at least 99.5% pure and is in the form of bars or ingots.

Don't be concerned about the difference between bars and ingots. The word ingot usually refers to a large bar of gold – like the ones you see in bank vaults. Everything else from the smallest pulled gold is referred to usually as a gold bar.

As far as coins are concerned, it all depends on your investment point of view. Unless you are extremely well off, gold coins are the usual way of owning gold. Most countries issue gold coins and yet, believe it or not, there are several countries which claim that their own coin is the fastest and biggest selling coin in the world depending on who you ask but the fact is that the South African Krugerrand accounts for about 50% of all coins currently languishing in people's portfolios!

Why would you want to invest in either coins or bars? Unlike saving money, gold should be regarded as an investment which you hold onto and do not buy and sell unless you absolutely have to. Many people, including the author started their investment portfolio in gold before moving on to equities and the whole of the panoply of investments available.

Think of investing in gold bullion as a starting point. It is a universally traded commodity and once you have an investment portfolio, it should be the last thing that you dispose of.

Think of it in the same way that you think about your house – not as an investment but as a possession. It is the best form of financial insurance that you could ever have.

Having said all that, there may well be a time when the price of gold skyrockets and then of course you may wish to seriously think about disposing of some... but we shall discuss that later.

It is also worth mentioning that if you buy gold for investment purposes, it is not only VAT- free but also free of Stamp Duty – if you are in the European Union. That is as a result of the 2000 EU gold directive.

You should also note that most of the traded gold coins are not 24 carat gold but only 91.7%, 22 carat. That is for the very practical reason of giving them a certain amount of strength by the addition of another metal. That is simply to protect them and harden them against wear because they do tend to be handled a lot more than gold bars. However you will find that they do contain the correct and stated weight of gold with some additional weight from the added metal.

The UK Britannia coin as well as the South African Krugerrand and the American Eagle fall into the 22 carat category.

Nevertheless, there are other coins which can be referred to as bullion coins which are 99.99%, 24 carat without any additions. They include the Australian Dragon, the Canadian Maple Leaf and the Chinese Panda. Look out for those if you're determined only to collect pure gold.

The only other thing worth mentioning at this stage is that it is cheaper to buy bullion rather than coin because there are fewer attached costs.

There is another class of coin which I think is worth mentioning and that is the collectors' coin. The so-called numismatic and rare coin is bought not only for the gold value but also for the aesthetic or historical value as well as the rarity. The interesting fact about this type of coin is that because of the other factors involved in the evaluation, they tend to rise faster than the gold price itself when the gold price is increasing in a bull market. However the converse is also true and they tend to lose value faster than a coin priced simply on its gold value in a bear market – when prices are falling.

The most preferred size of gold coin, no matter of what nationality contains 1 ounce of metal.

Finally, always be careful because there are some very unscrupulous people around and sad to say it is not unusual to come across fake gold coins. They're reasonably easy to spot because you can bend them in half because they are no more than gold-plated lead.

There is a modern trend for companies to issue all sorts of medals and pretend coins, citing them to be 'limited editions'. Yes, they do have a value but unfortunately once you pay for the box and the marketing, you are paying far more than just the intrinsic value of the gold and it is always doubtful whether these limited editions are a good way of investing – unless of course you are keen on solid gold coins depicting, for instance, birds of the world or American presidents!

This type of product comes under the general heading of 'Gold Rounds' – which in reality is what they are. Many of these products come in brilliant form - that is to say that the gold is very pure. There is no typical weight for these round pieces of gold but they do have the great advantage of often being cheaper to buy than gold coins because unlike official coins, they do not have to be made by a government mint. That means that they tend to have fewer overhead costs.

Before we look at specific gold coins, the first thing that you should remember as a new investor is only to buy from a reputable source, look out for fakes and only invest cash that you can afford to invest.

Let's have a look at a few specific coins:
The Krugerrand is the daddy of all gold coins and still represents a huge chunk of the gold coin market. It is produced by the South African Mint and has been in circulation since 1967.

Because of its longevity, all gold dealers know it as do most investors. It only took 13 years from inception for the Krugerrand to represent about 90% of the world's gold market.

As you may know, South Africa is one of the world's major producers of mined gold and when the Krugerrand was first minted, South Africa was the major gold producer. Production levels have varied over the years, depending on supply and demand, notably during the time when Western countries suddenly became aware of apartheid and as a protest, decreed that Krugerrands could not be imported or traded.

Fortunately, those days have now gone although the levels of the early 70s when 200,000 coins were minted in one year have not been recaptured and current production is of the order of 25 to 30,000 coins per annum. Single-handedly, the Krugerrand gave a private individuals the ability to invest in gold without having to buy expensive jewellery.

South Africa used the Krugerrand purely as a way of marketing their gold without having to go through the processes of creating jewellery. That meant that private individuals could now buy small amounts of gold in the knowledge that the value of their coin could be very simply calculated on a day-to-day basis.

The Krugerrand was also produced as legal tender. That is to say it formed part of South Africa's currency. Because it was produced for circulation, it was minted as 22 carat and is in fact a gold/copper alloy. Just as an example of its popularity; in the 10 years leading up to 1985, 22 million Krugerrands were imported into the United States.

The Krugerrand contains one Troy ounce of gold although it weighs 1.0909 Troy ounces. The difference is made up of the added copper.

It is also worth mentioning that the Krugerrand has been copied, so before you start buying Krugerrand do familiarise yourself with the coin. In order to stay within the law, many companies have minted what looks like a Krugerrand to the untrained eye and in fact only contains slight variations.

As stated above, always check the weight of the Krugerrand (over one Troy ounce), with the exact dimensions of a 32.77 mm diameter and the thickness of 2.84mm.

Many of the Krugerrand replicas are minted to the correct dimensions but the weight will vary.

You will also come across smaller Krugerrands which are ½, ¼, 1/10 ounces. They were introduced as far back as 1980 and also minted in 22 carat gold.

It is also worth mentioning that Krugerrands have 160 serrations around the edge and Proof Krugerrands have to 220. (Proof Krugerrands were produced as more of a collector's item than an investment and they are valued slightly above the bullion price).

At about the peak production time of the Krugerrand in the early to mid-80s, various other countries jumped on the gold bandwagon with America introducing the American Gold Eagle, the United Kingdom introducing the Britannia. The Australian Nugget and the Canadian Gold Maple Leaf as well as the Chinese Panda also appeared during these years.

The Britannia

Although they would doubtless deny it, the gold Britannia coin was first introduced in the United Kingdom by the Royal Mint in 1987, as a direct result of the success of the Krugerrand.

The Britannia was initially introduced as one Troy ounce of gold, initially with the exact make-up of a Krugerrand, that is to say 22 carat gold, and alloyed with copper. Three years later the copper was substituted for silver. If you put one of the original Britannia coins next to one since 1990 you will see a subtle colour difference. The original ones are somewhat yellower than the ones containing silver.

Just like the Krugerrand, the Britannia coin can be obtained in all sorts of denominations ranging from the 1 ounce right down to the 12 mm, 1.58 g, and 1/20 ounce coin.

If you come across a coin which was minted since 2013, you are no longer dealing with a 22 carat gold coin but with .9999 purity, that is to say 24 carat. In addition there was a new coin introduced in 2003 to coincide with Queen Elizabeth's 60th anniversary of being on the British throne. During that year, a 5 ounce coin was introduced which has a face value of £500 plus a tiny one with a face value of £5.

In truth, whether you buy the Krugerrand, the American Eagle or the Britannia makes no difference because what you are buying is the gold – but nowadays there is a certain element of patriotism attached to gold buying so your local dealer will no doubt be encouraging you to buy the local coins!

When buying Britannia coins or seeing quotes for them, beware because there is also a full set in Sterling Silver. You can buy Britannia coins in boxes, in pouches and in plastic holders etc. with the British Royal Mint's marketing department working very hard to persuade us to part with our cash.

If you are going to invest in Britannia coins, buy them direct from the Royal Mint. Nowadays, you can even pay for them by credit or debit card online and expect delivery within a day or so.

If you buy direct from the Royal Mint, there is little chance of you being fooled by a gold-plated silver Britannia or any of the other scams which are available!

The Sovereign

In Great Britain in the olden days, it was the Sovereign that people turned to as an investment. That is because the word Sovereign has been in the English language for about 600 years and although the current coin has little similarity to the original English Sovereign, from a marketing and name awareness point of view, it has few rivals.

In fact right up to 1932, it was in circulation as a proper coin of the realm. It has a nominal value of 1 pound sterling.

In the United Kingdom it is not unusual to see a gold Sovereign mounted as a pendant and is often worn, even to this day.

Although the original English gold Sovereign was last amended in 1604, it was resurrected in 1816 with a weight of .235420 Troy ounces... and the modern Sovereign continued to be produced to that particular specification.

What makes the Sovereign quite universal is the fact that it was not only minted by the British Royal Mint but for a time it was also minted in South Africa, Australia and Canada. Nowadays it is almost exclusively minted by the Royal Mint of Wales with a much smaller volume of coins being produced in India.

As is the usual practice with these valuable coins, there are other denominations. Apart from the original and standard pound Sovereign, there is also a half Sovereign, a double Sovereign and quintuple Sovereign, although it is only the Sovereign and the half Sovereign which used to be minted for circulation.
Just like the Krugerrand, the Sovereign is 22 carat that is the same 91.6% pure and has a diameter of 22.05 mm and a thickness of 1.52 mm. This is been the standard since 1817.

As with most coins, Sovereigns are not always collected for the intrinsic value but also for numismatic purposes because over the years, there have been certain variants, depending where and when the coins were minted.

About 1 billion Sovereigns have been minted over the years and as they have been used for intergovernmental payment of debt, many of them have been melted down and recycled as gold bars. In fact in 1933 when the coins were withdrawn from circulation, many were melted down and converted.

One thing you should be aware of is the fact that the weight of the coin which has been its regulation is quite critical. For instance the standard weight of the Sovereign expressed in metric terms is 7.98805 g. For it to remain legal tender, allowing for the wear that any coin experiences during circulation with the consequent weight loss, the minimum weight allowable for a Sovereign to remain as legal tender is 7.93787 g. Bear this in mind when you are purchasing them.

Lucky however even 100 years ago, although legal, it was not normal practice for coins to be circulated in the way that we understand it nowadays. Unless you were extremely rich, you would be very unlikely to dip into your pocket for a handful of change and find several Sovereigns in there. Luckily even in those days most Sovereigns would be kept either in a home safe or a bank vault.

1891 was a crucial date in the life of the original Sovereign because the government was aware that gold was being hoarded and in 1891, it was decreed that any gold coins struck before 1837 were no longer legal tender which meant that the coins were ordered to be returned to the Royal Mint where they were melted down and re-minted as new Sovereigns and half Sovereigns.

1914 was beginning of World War I and that was also the time when the United Kingdom ceased to use the gold standard. That meant that the Royal Mint no longer produced Sovereigns but they were still minted offshore – again in South Africa, Australia, India and Canada.

Coins were counterfeited during this period, notably in Italy, especially between 1932 and when production restarted in the UK in 1957.

The rather muddled history of the Sovereign continued with it being produced until 1982 when, instead of being produced as bullion, only proof coins were produced. Nowadays, since the turn of the millennium, we are back to bullion Sovereigns being produced at the Royal Mint in Wales.

Although Sovereigns are produced on a regular basis, it has always been the practice not to apply that particular year's date to a coin. For instance, Sovereigns produced nowadays, have the date of 2010 and those produced during the reign of King George the sixth were still all dated 1925 and featured George V!

Not only are the dates confusing, although the actual age of a coin does not matter unless you are a coin collector, the specific number of coins minted in the year is also some form of state secret so it is very difficult to ascertain exactly how many coins have been produced, bearing in mind that many have been melted down and recycled as either gold bars or other Sovereigns.

The modern day purchasing power of a gold Sovereign is over £100, in spite of the fact that its original face value is one pound sterling.

If you do decide to buy any gold coin, especially the Sovereign, be aware not only of counterfeiting but other techniques which are used in order to decrease the weight of the coin.

The first one is known as 'sweating' and is a process where a lot of gold coins are placed in a leather bag and shaken for a time. Because of the nature of the metal, the friction between the coins produces gold dust which is then collected and needless to say, all the coins are slightly lighter.

The softness of the metal also allows yet another technique to be used to reduce the weight of the coin. This is done by using a blade to cut up small slivers of the coin and then 'hammering' gently in order to conceal the fact that part of the coin has been cut off. Otherwise, small holes can be drilled both around the perimeter and into the coin itself with the resulting swarf being collected and the holes being concealed once again by gentle hammering, usually with a small hammer and a flat-ended punch.

Always be on your guard when purchasing coins, especially from a private individual or online. Once again, you should get to know your coins intimately, and you should invest in a scale as well as a gauge so as to measure the thickness and the diameter. Also bear in mind that coins which have been in circulation for a while or have been handled over the years will have naturally lost some of their weight. I have indicated the lower limit above.

In olden times, it was also common practice to cut bits out of coins as payment but nowadays it is very rare to find a coin which has been treated in this way, except perhaps in a museum.

If a coin has been counterfeited from either a gold alloy or possibly plated lead, the dimensions will not be wildly different but you will find that these coins tend to be thicker with a larger diameter.

If you are a coin collector, you should also be aware of the fact that there are counterfeiters who produce coins with exactly the same amount of gold that creates either ancient versions of the coin or as a rare mintage. Spotting those only comes with experience.

As you know many antique dealers and jewellers, collect old gold and melt it down. You will not be surprised therefore that it is not unknown for unscrupulous members of both professions to produce

9 carat 'Sovereigns' as well as other coins... but as you know by now, it's all to do with the weight/size ratio.

As with all gold coins, Sovereigns are made in 22 carat gold, plus a single copper alloy in order to make them slightly harder and more robust although you may be lucky enough to find an early Australian-produced Sovereign which contains silver instead of copper.

Although, the Sovereign is not as widely collected as an investment as say, the Krugerrand, it is probably the most popular coin collected by numismatists... primarily as a result of its long and colourful history.

I know of many people who have entered the gold investment market via the Sovereign or half-Sovereign, so it is a coin well worth getting to know!

North American Coins
There are only two coins of current importance, and they represent practically 100% of the North American market. In North America, it is the Canadian Maple Leaf and the American Eagle which are by far the easiest to buy and sell. The two coins are 24 carat and 22 carat respectively. In order to compete with a 24 carat Canadian coin, the US Mint introduced the American Buffalo in 2006 but it is not as popular as the American Eagle, and the odds are that you haven't even heard of it.

The American Eagle is claimed to be the world's best-selling gold coin and on occasions it has been. It is certainly growing in popularity – especially since the advent of the Internet. You can not only buy coins direct from the American Mint but in common with many other coins you can buy privately on the Internet – but do beware for the reasons stated above. There are many fakes about!

The American Eagle is a 1 ounce coin and it comes in four denominations with a ½ ounce, a ¼ ounce and the 1/10th also available.

In keeping with the general advice I would give to all prospective gold investors, stick with 1 ounce coins because the smaller denomination coins still have a premium attached to them, so if you collect the smaller denomination coins you will find that the premiums are not calculated on a pro rata basis which means that when you end up with a collection of lower denomination coins, the premium you would have paid would be far higher than had you stuck with 1 ounce coins.

One of things that I have seen in the American market is that there seems to be quite a lively trade in 'rare' American Eagles. Avoid them. These coins require far more expertise than the average investor has and by the time you have had a particular coin inspected by an expert or by a professional grading service, your costs will have risen which rather defeats the object of being a bona fides investor.

Buying any rare coin is more an art than a science and although many rare coins do have a value which can be a multiple of the actual gold value, they are best avoided.

The **Canadian Gold Maple Leaf** is made of pure gold, that is to say 24 carat and has a face value of $50 Canadian dollars, although it does come in smaller denominations as well as the standard one Troy ounce. The other denominations are the 1/25th oz, 1/20th oz, 1/10th oz ¼ oz and ½ oz.

For the generally available pure gold coins, it is the most purchased, although there have been many complaints from investors about the fact that they do tend to wear very easily. That of course is a function of the metal which has been previously discussed.

The coin was introduced in 1979 when the only other available for investment was the Krugerrand. It was an excellent marketing ploy by the Royal Canadian Mint because at that time the politicians were tightly focused on the apartheid in South Africa and made it difficult for individuals outside of South Africa to buy the Krugerrand.

Of all the bullion coins, the Canadian Gold Maple Leaf has the most variants and currently it appears to change year-on-year and unfortunately it is not within the scope of this book to tell you about every single one but the information is readily available on the Internet.

As a matter of interest, in 2007, the Royal Canadian Mint produced a Gold Maple Leaf coin 50 cm in diameter by 3 cm thick, weighing 100 kg. The nominal face value was $1 million but needless to say it is now worth four or five times that amount.

The Royal Canadian Mint, above all others is very keen on producing boxed sets and once again if you are keen on investing in pure gold, be aware of the expense of the sometimes extravagant packaging.

Each Canadian Gold Maple Leaf has a portrait of Queen Elizabeth II of England on one side.

Bearing in mind the many mintings and variations in the Canadian Gold Maple Leaf coin, it is an excellent vehicle for those who are interested in both the gold and just enjoy collecting coins.

As far as buying *any* coins is concerned I would suggest two things: the first is buying on eBay, because you're going to involve yourself in a bid contest and maybe end up paying over the odds. Secondly is to shop around because some traders and dealers will charge you a 5% premium. Try and avoid any premium if you can.

Industrial Gold

As you probably realise, one of the great problems of the rapidly accelerating the **electronics** industry is the fact that battery technology is still very primitive and no one has yet found a way to store electricity.

If you own a smartphone you know that you need to charge it at least once a day and electronics manufacturers continue to work very hard to try and extend battery life. They do this in two main ways. The first is to design circuitry which works at lower and lower voltages and currents so that battery life is preserved for as long as possible. The second is to use the very best materials with the best conductive qualities.

However to achieve this, circuits have to be not only conducting electricity as efficiently as possible but because most metals are prone to corrosion, the flow of electricity can easily be interrupted by the minutest corrosion in a circuit.

That is why the industry needs a metal which is an efficient conductor of electricity which does not oxidise.

The metal which meets these criteria is gold. That means that the more you move into the virtual reality and smartphone revolution, the more gold is going to be required by the industry.

Connectors which connect memory chips onto a computer motherboard contain gold as do male and female connectors used to attach cables. All these components are not solid gold by any means but they are either alloyed to conducting metals or more commonly, plated onto other alloys.

Therefore in the long term, because of the finite nature of the gold available, it is a metal with a future.

Gold has also been used in **dentistry** for a very long time-again because of the fact that it is non-corrosive as well as having a certain aesthetic appeal in some quarters – although the fashion of having a front gold tooth has dissipated somewhat in later years.

The other great attraction for dentists is the fact that because of this malleability, gold crowns etc. are very easy for the dentist to work with.

The earliest known use of gold in dentistry was about 1000 years ago when gold wire was used to fasten replacement teeth. Gold was also used in ancient times to fill cavities in teeth.

Currently it is still used in alloy form for crowns, fillings, and bridges. Needless to say, for durability, it is alloyed with various other metals but in such a way as to not affect the metals non-allergenic properties.

There are various uses of gold in medicine. For instance radioactive gold isotopes are implanted in people as a radiation source in order to treat certain cancers.

Certain gold compounds are used in the treatment of rheumatoid arthritis and a very unusual use of gold is in the treatment of a condition which results in the patient not being able to close his or her eyes. Small amounts of gold are implanted into the upper eyelid. This weighs down the eyelid, enabling the patient's eyes to function normally.

The last 20 years have seen a vast acceleration in the use of electronic equipment in medicine and of course as stated above, every single piece of apparatus contains some gold within the electronic circuitry.

Even surgical instruments nowadays contain a small amount of gold.

So once again, as an investment, it has a bright future in the medical industry

Gold continues to be used in the **glassmaking** industry. You may be surprised to know that when small amounts of gold are added to glass and when the glass is annealed, it turns to a ruby colour.

You may also have seen skyscrapers with slightly gold tinted windows. Gold is used in glass as a coating which reflects solar radiation from the outside and reflects the frequencies inwards. The same principle is used on **astronauts'** visors.

Speaking of astronauts, the various buggies used by astronauts as well as the remote robots that have been sent to Mars have a high gold content apart from the obvious one within the electronic circuitry. The lubrication of mechanical parts in space is achieved with gold because of its 'slip' properties, as ordinary organic as well as synthetic oil will be totally destroyed by the radiation of space.

The amazing malleability of gold means that it has been used by **furniture** makers as well as **architects** to adorn all manner of objects for many hundreds of years. If you think of the Cathedral of the Moscow Kremlin or any number of churches in Europe and even the Far East, there are hundreds of examples of gold leafing – and gold leaf continues to be used as a roofing material in certain cases.

Jewellery

Apart from the practical uses shown above, and its collectability as well as its excellent investment properties, gold has always been a status symbol and an expression of success.

That is why the winner of an event at the Olympic Games receives a *gold* medal, rather than an iron or copper one (although since the beginning of the 20th century, Olympic medals contain a very small percentage of gold!).

Gold has become synonymous with being 'Number 1'.

The King or Queen of a country does not wear a crown unless it is made of gold! That's because of gold association with status.

Its association with purity and hence being the metal of choice in the production of most religious artefacts gives any church service an added gravitas, although on many occasions it is seen as the churches expression of its wealth – that was not the initial intention.

The very first piece of jewellery or body adornment ever made from gold was probably fashioned from a nugget found in a stream or on the ground. Since those days, it is generally accepted that the best jewellery is made from gold and with the added value of the artistry and craftsmanship that goes into any piece of jewellery, jewellery is also viewed as an excellent investment.

If you do decide to invest in jewellery, do not buy it new from a jewellery shop. Buy your jewellery second-hand and do your best to negotiate a price based purely on the gold in order to exclude the premium which owners tend to add in respect of their emotional attachment and the aesthetic beauty of the piece.

However, when buying jewellery, do make sure that you are buying what you think you're buying. Remember the gold content of 9 carat gold is vastly different to 22 carat gold and all the golds in between!
If you are considering investing in jewellery, even if you intend to scrap it or have it melted down, invest in a book of hallmarks and never buy gold jewellery or gold without hallmarks or without a gold testing kit.

The final thing I shall say about investing in physical gold in any way shape or form, is to make sure that you are able to handle it at some stage and store it in a bank vault or in a strong box of some sort. Do not accept offers from dealers who will say that they will look after it for you and that it is safer to be left with them.

There are many ways of investing in nonphysical gold – that is to say gold that you cannot see, smell or touch and that is what we are going to be looking at next.

Chapter 3 – Paper Gold

Gold Miners & Gold Shares

Equities or shares in a company are very often the nearest investors ever come to a bar of gold. Just like the metal itself and in fact, this refers to any commodity, the price of shares in gold mines or gold is governed by supply and demand.

Miners all over the world are looking for investors and if you are interested in this type of investment, the first bit of advice I would give you is to study the company in detail, have a look at its previous performance (and not just the chairman's normally bullish statement and estimate of how much gold is going to be mined).

The equation is simple, investing is all about the future and if you find a mine that has been plodding along happily for many years with a good production record, and I have found that it is always worth investing in because you never know what is just around the corner. Having said that, it is very easy for a company to keep plodding along forever but every gold company I have come across issues the occasional bulletin which gives an indication of where they are exploring and the likelihood of any future finds – and recently, because of advances in technology, these predictions have become more and more accurate.

However remember, all you need is for a mine to suffer some form of catastrophe such as flooding, death, corruption, nationalisation and your shares in the company can be very adversely affected.

All you need to remember is the old adage that 'prices can go down as well as up'.

I shall give you a real example of a gold mine I invested in about two years ago because I noticed that its share price had suddenly dipped and then started to climb. I telephoned the company chief executive who told me that they'd had a massive cash injection. The rumour of the cash injection spread through the market and the share price multiplied very fast over a matter of two or three days. Luckily by then I had bought shares, waited until I'd quadrupled my initial investment and sold them, in spite of the fact that it looked as if the shares were going to remain on an upward trajectory. Just over one week later, the company announced that it was going into receivership. The cash injection that it had been given was an attempt to save it rather than a bona fide investment.

I was lucky on that occasion plus I do have a certain knowledge of equity investments so if you are going to invest in miners or shares of any kind, seek expert advice and certainly only invest a small portion of your portfolio.

Volatility is one of those things that gold has a habit of being used as a 'hedge' against. In later years, the price of gold has been quite volatile but be careful because gold shares and gold funds are based on mining rather than the end product which can be even more risky and volatile. So when looking at a mining company to invest in, one of the factors you should be looking at is the difference between the gold prices and how much it costs them to extract gold. It varies quite a lot from mine to mine.

Some mines are extracting gold on very tight margins which means that even if the price of gold drops a little they could find themselves in trouble with the share price plummeting unexpectedly. That is because the fall in the gold price is vastly amplified within any company share price if that company is working on very tight margins.

Gold Certificates & Unallocated Gold Accounts

Gold certificates and gold accounts are all about trusting the banks! No doubt bankers will take great exception to anyone even suggesting any possible impropriety but the fact is that mistakes have been made.

Let me explain about gold certificates and allocated gold accounts.

Instead of having a box full of gold or a safety deposit box in the bank containing coins and bars of gold, you can by a gold certificate from a bank which says that you own a certain volume of gold and very often it will even refer by serial number to the bars or whatever it is that you own. The gold is stored within a bank vault but it is nominally yours. Unsurprisingly, most people do not ask to see it although I do remember many years ago actually being asked by an investor who came into the branch wanting to see how his hard earned cash had been stored!

Therefore, an *allocated* gold certificate refers to gold that is specifically earmarked for you, the investor.

Unallocated gold certificates are all about owning what can best be described as part of a pool of gold but unlike allocated gold shares will not guarantee that you will have all of your investment returned in the event of a run on the banks gold.

The reason I express misgivings about this type of investment is only for the reason of having heard of a bank allocating the same gold to several different investors simultaneously which is not a problem if the investors redeem their gold in cash. But it could pose a problem if there was a run on the bank and you wanted to claim your gold bar!

Please do not worry about this type of investment, it is not common but it is still well worth knowing about. Fractional reserve banking (as it is known) is not for the fainthearted in case of any problems so for the moment I would suggest that you steer clear of it and stick to gold that you can see and touch.

I have covered unallocated gold in a later section even though I have always considered it as the nearest thing to a Ponzi Scheme that banks legally operate.

Exchange Traded Funds (ETFs)

ETFs were first introduced in 2003 and although I think it is important for you to understand what they are, I would certainly advise you to steer well clear of this type of investment.

Exchange traded products (ETPs) are designed by investors for professional investors rather than the man in the street. And they have the same aura about them as did those dreadful mortgage-backed securities which contributed so much to the banking crisis of 2008.

Just as you do with gold certificates, you invest in a pool of gold which is traded on the stock exchange in exactly the same way as equities. The most interesting thing about ETF's is the fact that they contain any number of charges from a management fee, insurance, storage to trading fees.

These charges are applied on a very regular basis so in a flat market the amount of gold shown on your certificate will gradually dissipate as charges are extracted from it. If you understand unit linked investment funds you will have a rough idea of how ETF's work. Suffice to say that you do not own a specific piece of gold anywhere but a non-specific unit within a large investment.

Derivatives Markets

If you are proper gambler, this may just be the type of gold investment that you are looking for.

If you've heard words such as 'futures' you know exactly what I'm talking about. It's all to do with risk – as is everything with an investment.

There are many commodities you can invest in with gold being one of the major ones and there are exchanges all over the world which specifically deal with this type of investment. Basically you are betting on what the gold price will be at some point in the future. Bearing in mind the global economic uncertainties, this may either be the best or the worst time to invest in gold, depending on your point of view!

Recently there have been problems with individuals and companies investing in gold futures and for various real or imaginary reasons their future contracts were not able to be executed because the gold which they had bought was not available when it should have been.

There are Gold Derivatives contracts which allow you to ask for settlement in physical gold and others which offer a cash settlement so that you never actually ever come into contact with any gold.

So the choice you have is gold futures and options which are denominated in a certain currency and designed to be cash settled with an option for physical delivery – which is usually purely theoretical. Very often the contracts are based on a specific weight of gold – typically one hundred Troy ounces. The price is the one fixed by the London bullion market and is the price taken as the reference for any cash settlement.

This type of investment is definitely one where you need an intermediary, obviously with the associated additional costs.

All these products are traded on exchanges all over the world, although you can also translate these deals over the counter in the private market.

Chapter 4 – Gold Investment

Spread Betting Gold Prices

Spread betting is very often one of those terms that anyone who is even vaguely interested in investment has heard but does not necessarily have a very clear understanding of what exactly it means and what it entails.

Spread betting differs from a normal wager in that you are predicting the outcome of an event. In this case it's going to be the price of gold.

Most investments have two prices one is the *Buying* (BID) price and the other is the *Selling* (OFFER) price. The buying price is higher than the selling price. The difference between the two prices is called "The Spread".

When you invest, you buy at the higher price and sell at the lower price.

A spread bet is when an investor (you or me) bets whether (in this case) the price of gold will be lower than the BID price or higher than the OFFER price. That means that you are not always betting and hoping for a higher price because you can quite easily make just as much from your investment when the prices fall.

You the investor, does not actually own any of the gold that you're going to be betting on but are merely speculating on the changes in the gold price – whether up or down.

Nowadays you can carry out this kind of 'bet' either face-to-face or via phone, Internet or even smartphone.

Let's say that today's gold price is 1100/1105. That means we can buy at 1105 and we sell at 1100 – although this does not apply in our case because we are just going to be considering the market.

We are in a rising market at the moment so we can assume that the buying price will go up from 1105.

So we place a bet at say £100 per point upwards from 1105... however we do have to be careful because once again, to repeat the old mantra 'Prices can go down as well as up'. That means that like any professional investor we will protect any possible downside. The reason for doing this is that if the price of gold drops and we're in for £100 per point, by the time we want to settle the debt, our losses could be substantial unless we place some sort of 'stop' on the bet in order to limit our losses.

If we place the stop at say 25 points from 1105 and the price goes down to 1080 that is the point at which the bet stops and any loss has been limited to £2500 – that is 25 points at £100 per point.

However as the market is rising, we keep an eye on the market until we think that the price has topped out and we take the profit.

Let's say that a month down the line, the price of gold has risen to 1200/1205. We decide to take profit which is going to be 1200-1105 x£100 (That's the new selling price minus the original price we bought at, multiplied by the bet of £100 per point).

That is 95 x £100, which gives us a profit of £9500.

Had we suspected that the gold price was going to go down, we could have carried out exactly the same calculation that using the reverse Bid/Offer numbers.

Spread betting is not for the fainthearted and unsurprisingly vast fortunes have been made and vast fortunes have been lost.

The great advantage is that you can make a profit no matter what the market is doing. The divisive placing a stop on the downside means that although you limit yourself on the losses, your profits can be as high as you let them or until you lose your nerve!

If you want to have a look at this market, you will need to go to a spread betting broker.

All you need is a broker, cash and a decision whether to place an up bet or a down bet and of course how much you wish to bet per point.

Investors who deal in vast amounts of money, are able to make huge profits through very small movements in the price.

Normal practice is to put in a stop loss order at about the Bid/Offer spread, that is to say either the bid or offer price, depending whether your bet is up or down.

I would also advise you to call your broker and ask what the minimum bet is, so that you can practice without doing too much potential damage to your bank balance

Tips for Investing in Gold

The very first thing that I'm going to say in this section is that you should learn to walk before you run.

Traditionally gold (or specifically *physical* gold) should be in the same category as your house as far as your portfolio is concerned. It is not something that you should trade on a daily basis. On the contrary it is something that you should be prepared to hold onto for at least a number of years.

There are many opportunities for short to mid-term investment with gold as shown in the previous sections.

The price of gold is influenced by many factors including things such as the global economy as well as the more mundane supply and demand and even currency fluctuations. Traditionally, gold is the one commodity that speculators will run to when they see trouble coming.

Of course the gold price is also influenced by speculation, and this is becoming more and more of a factor in calculating its day-to-day price.

The International Monetary Fund as well as major central banks also play an important role in fixing the gold price, as they hold more than 20% of the entire world's reserves. Surprisingly though, apparently very healthy economies such as China only hold of the order of 1.5% of their national reserves in gold. Of course as soon as the market begins to suspect that China is about to go on a gold buying spree, prices will inevitably rise.

India is another vast consumer of gold and much of it is held in private hands but nevertheless with the rise in its population and its current economic growth, its appetite for gold appears insatiable. Two years ago for instance India bought about 200 tonnes of gold which caused a spike in gold prices.

In addition, there has been talk of interest-rate rises in the West. The USA has already lifted its rates by a small amount and other countries such as the United Kingdom look as if they are going to follow suit. Historically, the gold price has risen when interest rates have risen. So currently it is well worth keeping an ear open for what politicians are saying, especially as in many cases they are much clumsier than professional dealers as far as gold is concerned.

For instance a few years ago, the British Prime Minister Gordon Brown *announced* that he was going to sell some of the United Kingdom's gold – in fact it was a large proportion of it. Speculators, realising that several tonnes of gold were suddenly going to appear on the market at the same time caused prices to tumble so that by the time the hapless Mr Brown sold the United Kingdom's gold, the price had plummeted.

If you are genuinely interested in investing in gold, I would certainly begin by purchasing a few coins and taking it from there, maybe moving onto small bars but trying to listen all the time. The price of gold in bars is usually less than coins but the downside is that as I have stated several times, there are thousands of gold forgeries out there. The inevitable advice therefore is that you should stick to buying gold from reputable sources.

In principle it is very easy. Start looking at the gold price on a day-to-day basis. If it's headed down, read as much information as you can and try and ascertain the reasons why it is going down. Then you can make a decision as to whether it's gone down as far as it is going to – and that is the time to buy! Obviously if you are in selling mood you wait for the price to rise as far as possible.

Once again I would remind you to remember to distinguish between the different purities and if you can, learn the various hallmarks and indicators of purity.

Obviously I have no idea which tax regime you the reader is in, but in general, gold is treated very favourably from a VAT and other taxation point of view.

So, all you need to do is to get into the habit of some day-to-day analysis which is available to everyone nowadays. All the charts, market trends, moving averages, opinion and details about your own countries economy are all clearly published so you have all the information at your fingertips to join in this very exciting and often lucrative market.

Chapter 5 – Virtual Gold

Digital Gold Currency

Yes I know that after the 2008 financial crisis, anything with the word 'digital' and 'currency' tends to make one stop and take notice. However digital gold currency does exist and it is very straightforward and it is no more than a private currency which is backed by gold bullion.

There are companies which provide this type of currency thus making it possible for you to own gold and buy and sell gold but without the aggravation of storage or worrying about security. It has been specifically designed for online transactions and that of course is its only use. The value of your gold obviously fluctuates with the official gold price.

If you explore digital gold currency accounts, you will notice that the balances and transactions are expressed in weight rather than a symbol.

The advantage of digital gold is that it can be purchased in any weight unlike bars or coins which come in physical predetermined amounts.

Unallocated Gold Accounts

I have already covered the principle of unallocated gold accounts together with all the dangers in respect of the possibility of runs on a holding bank and the position in the queue of holders of unallocated gold.

However, I thought that I would add a few additional facts about unallocated gold because it does come under the heading of virtual gold – in the sense that it doesn't really exist. No doubt banks would argue with this conclusion but let me explain:

Firstly, unallocated gold is by far the most common way for individuals to invest in gold. They do so very often in the mistaken belief that they are buying physical gold usually because the bank which issues a certificate does not actually tell them that the gold that they are buying is not somehow kept in a vault ready for them to claim at sometime in the future. But from an ownership point of view, it is even more complicated than that.

I have already said that when you buy unallocated gold, it is you who is accepting the risk should the bank ever have a liquidity problem - and although 50 years ago the mere thought of the bank having a liquidity problem was a pretty wild thought, events of the last 10 years or so certainly show that banks are not as safe as we once thought. In spite of all the legislation and the compliance regimes which have sprung up all over the place, banks are still indulging in shall we say, creative accounting designed to advantage the bank books themselves rather than their customers.

The first thing you should know is that if you buy unallocated gold, you become a creditor of the bank. That is to say you do not own the gold but the bank owes it to you. Meanwhile, you are thinking *"I have invested in gold and the bank is looking after it for me… how safe is that?"*

You sign an agreement with the bank and therefore on paper, you are a gold depositor! Not only that but for the privilege of having gold, you are charged a fee above the golds spot price.

As you have probably read, nowadays banks are required by law to hold a certain proportion of their liabilities in assets which are capable of being turned into cash immediately and it has been designed to protect the bank in the event of a run when depositors want their money out at more or less the same time.

One of the assets which is highly regarded as being suitable for converting quickly into cash is gold. Unfortunately that means that if the bank does have some gold, represented by the document you are holding, and if it is unallocated, on the bank's balance sheet, it is considered not yours but part of the banks reserve.

So you can see therefore, that unallocated gold is a great way for a bank to comply with the law and maintain its liquidity.

You have handed the bank cash for your unallocated gold and not only is the bank able to use the money you have given them, the gold that you have paid for is added in its reserve.

That means that if there was a run on the bank, the unallocated gold that you notionally own would be one of the first assets to be ditched and converted to cash, in spite of the fact that you are technically a bank creditor. As such, you are only in line to receive not the full amount of your investment necessarily but a proportion of what the bank can raise from any fire sale which unfortunately includes your unallocated gold.

That means that in buying unallocated gold, you are in danger of not reviving the full value of the gold you think you have bought, because what you have really bought into is all of the bank's assets which include the gold.

You may also have heard of the various depositor protection schemes up to a specific amount which governments have introduced and underwritten in order to protect depositors. The bad news is that any depositor protection scheme does not refer to what is technically a bullion debt.

In other words, rather than investing in unallocated gold, your best bet would be to put your money on deposit. Okay, the potential growth is nowhere near as you might achieve through investing in nominal gold but by investing in unallocated gold, you are not protecting any possible downside... and it is generally agreed that the banking catastrophes of 2008 will happen again!

If there is another banking catastrophe with subsequent runs on bank deposits, you will be among the last in the queue because you have no protection whatsoever in spite of the fact that you have contributed generously to the banks liquidity reserve.

If you are going to be making a choice between allocated an unallocated gold, I would recommend that you go the allocated route in spite of the banks additional charges in respect of 'storage' for allocated gold. The additional charge, usually of the order of 1.5% is there purely to encourage you to go the allocated route where the 'storage' is free.

Banks are not the only ones playing the unallocated game – even coin manufacturers seek investment into unallocated gold so that it is you the private investor who funds their inventory and their own purchases of gold.

Amazingly, 95% of the world's gold investment is in unallocated gold which means rather paradoxically, you invest in gold without ever seeing it and without having the security of actually owning it.

Chapter 6 – The Gold Middle Man

Comparing Dealers

Needless to say, there are good dealers, there are incompetent dealers and there are bandits.

You may already have been subjected to aggressive marketing campaigns by various gold experts who are telling you that by the end of next year, gold is going to climb to above $4000 an ounce and that they have predicted every single rise and fall of gold since time immemorial and that you should send them some money!

It is very easy to be seduced by such marketing, and many have been. I'm not for one moment suggesting that they have had their money stolen by these operators but in most cases, any cash that they have made has been nowhere near what was promised. Nevertheless these 'experts' meanwhile use the cash to make themselves a fortune. That is why so many of them are incredibly rich and not through their 'mediumship'.

As usual, I would suggest that if something sounds too good to be true, then it probably is and you should not be parting with your money as a result of either being emailed or contacted through the post with promises of untold riches by 'experts' who claim to be advisers to governments and who have never ever been wrong.

There are directories of gold brokers and the vast majority of them are respectable well-established companies, some of which have been active for many years. These are the ones that you should be going to. Beware of simply going to the dealer who is going to charge you the least.

Banks provide investment advice but I can say with hand on heart that I have found this to be very patchy, especially for the reasons I have described above in their treatment and explanation of unallocated gold.

As usual the very best people to go to are the ones that have been recommended to you. If you are thinking of investing in gold that suggests that you have a reasonable sum of money available so do your research before you part with a single penny.

Be especially wary of online dealers because quite a few have sprung up over the last few years, especially since 2008 when people don't trust their banks as much as they used to. If you do go to an online dealer, do make sure that you are buying gold and that at least they do have access to gold. Having said that, it is the Internet which gives you the sort of choice that we only used to dream about 25 years ago.

Remember the gold dealers are in it for the profit and they do it very simply – by buying for less than the market price and selling above the market price. The so-called 'spread' between the two prices is what they exist on. The spread varies appreciably and not only depends on the broker but also on the quantity and type of gold that you buy.

It is widely acknowledged that Hong Kong dealers are the best ones to buy gold coins from because they charge as little as 0.2% above the premium. You won't find dealers getting anywhere near that in the UK.

When you are selling your gold however, you will soon learn that you will find yourself on the wrong end of the bid/offer spread and be prepared to lose up to 5% of the market price.

Gold dealers are definitely the best people to go to in order to buy gold and finally I would just like to mention one thing which I have seen springing up over the last few years. It is those ubiquitous vending machines which tempt individuals to 'invest 'in gold by dispensing overpriced gold bars. Stay away from them.

Buyback Promises & Schemes

Many amateur gold buyers both buy and sell their gold at the wrong time because all they want to do is invest in gold without always looking at prices and very often there are times when they need to sell, which never seems to be at the right time.

One of the great advantages of buying from a bona fide gold dealer is the fact that most of them will have a buyback promise which means that you do not have the hassle of trying to sell your gold should you need to.

However, do have a close look at how much a buyback promise from a dealer is going to cost you.

The above is what is generally accepted as an explanation of 'buyback' but in recent times what used to be merely a service has been marketed as a scheme.

This is how a Gold buyback scheme might work: an investor purchases gold from a company for a small discount – and can even take the gold home if he wishes to do so. Meanwhile, the company has offered to buy that gold back at the original sale price after a specific time period, irrespective of the gold price at the time of buyback.

So far so good, and it all seems above board!

Assuming that the original discount was say 2%, the investor thinks that they will make a 2% profit because the company has offered to purchase back at the original pre-discount price.

In fact, the original discounted price would have been even higher than the price the gold would have been offered for to say banks or goldsmiths. That means that the investor is paying more for the gold than he would have in a straight purchase.

Some investors have been known to pay a premium of as much as 30% at the beginning of the deal. In addition, many of these buyback schemes have gone bankrupt, leaving investors in even more trouble.

There is no such thing as a free lunch.

Disadvantages of Investing in Gold

After all that I have said about gold as an investment, you may be imagining that there cannot be any disadvantages to investing in gold if you are wary and do your research properly... but I want to look at this in a more general way.

Gold has earned a very good reputation over the many years that we have dealt with it. It has many advantages - from its appearance and its intrinsic value to the fact that it appears to have bailed out the mismanagement of many economies by incompetent politicians.

I just want to look at it from a serious investor's point of view.

You should be aware of the fact that unlike many other investments, gold does not provide you with an income. If you have a few thousand dollars available, you may be better investing it in something else or merely putting it on deposit for a small return.

Neither will gold necessarily provide you with capital appreciation. Contrary to all the rumours, if you look at gold prices over the years, it is a very volatile investment – but in spite of that, it has gained a reputation as being 'rock solid'.

The way gold is valued, has always been subjective to a certain extent and there have been many attempts to fix the gold price to all sorts of other factors and it has to be said that so far, without success.

You may be interested to know, that currently it costs roundabout $550 to produce 1 ounce of gold. If the price of gold were to tend towards that amount, it would not be worth producing and you can work out for yourself what would happen to the gold price if production stopped – or can you?!

You should also remember that there is still a vast volume of gold still in the ground and in the sea. What would happen to the gold price if someone suddenly discovered a method for extracting it efficiently from seawater?

If you look back 40 years to the 1970s, you may remember that there was massive increase in the price of gold but in the following 20 years, it lost 80% of its value.

One of the great unknowns at the moment is the global economy, especially the anticipated performances of both the United States and China. Gold is certainly seen as a hedge against a weak US dollar and against inflation, but even economists have found both very difficult to predict plus now we have the central banks latest craze of quantitative easing which once again is an additional and non-predictable factor.

If you are gambling on the gold price, you are also gambling on what politicians are going to do next. Currently it is *their* actions which are affecting the price of gold the most.

In the last 10 years, the price of gold has tripled and in fact has doubled in the last six to seven years which suggests that the current volatility is primarily affected by speculative demand... and speculative demand is a very transient phenomenon which can go into reverse at any time.

So hopefully you can see, that gold is not the universal panacea that it was once thought to be and you should treat it with the same caution that you treat any other commodity or investments which you are considering.

Chapter 7 – Gold: The Big Picture

Credit Cycle and the Gold Price

A credit cycle is the name given to the periods in a business cycle when money is easy to borrow and gradually switching to a period when money is not so easy to borrow as was recently exemplified by the so-called 'credit' crunch which began in 2008.

The two parts of the cycle occur as follows: the 'UP' part of the cycle is usually accompanied by lower interest rates plus lower lending criteria as well as an increase in the amount of money that is available for people to borrow.

The 'DOWN' part of the cycle is the mirror image and the economy sees higher interest rates, tighter lending criteria and a decrease in the money supply.

Economists tend to argue about the causes but lately it has become apparent that two of the primary causes are economic mismanagement by politicians coupled with financial mismanagement by bankers.

The credit cycle affects the gold price in a very direct and predictable way. In general terms, the price of gold rises during the down part of the cycle as investors run for cover. Again in general terms, it is a time when equities tend to fall.

In spite of politicians positive predictions, especially in the United States and the United Kingdom, many economists believe that we are about to enter another down cycle. For instance, worldwide in 2015 there were nearly $80 billion worth of corporate debt defaults – the highest number of such defaults for six years.

This is not very good signal as far as the global economy is concerned. China is currently (2016) experiencing problems with its equity markets with an increasingly uncertain economic outlook, further amplified by the maintained drop-in oil price as well as the troubles in the Middle East.

Traditionally, this is a time when the price of gold begins to creep upwards.

Gold Scams

There are as many gold scams available as there are ways of investing in gold. Needless to say all are designed to part the gullible investor with his or her hard earned money. Let's have a look at some of the more common scams.

If you receive some shiny marketing literature which has an over preponderance of pictures of gold bars and gold coins on it, be very careful. There is a class of products known as an HYIP which stands for high yield investment programme and it is hinted that the scheme is 'backed' by investment in gold.

The routine is very simple, you send them money with an understanding that you will be able to redeem your investment at any time with a profit (always exaggerated!). They will tell you that you are investing in gold and they will probably be showing you graphs of how gold has risen over the last few years. So what can go wrong?

The fact is that many of these HYIPs are no more than Ponzi schemes. If anyone invests and then wants to take their money out, they will get their money but that money does not come from any gold investment but from the money invested by subsequent people into the scheme. If you recall the name Bernie Madoff, you know exactly what I'm talking about.

Beware of marketing literature which is slightly too shiny!

I have already mentioned fraudulent dealers selling counterfeit gold coins. In the gold market that is by far the most common form of fraud so if you do intend to participate in the coin bullion market, do your homework and as I described above buy a few bits of basic equipment, ranging from a Vernier calliper to a small set of electronic scales.

I know of several private individuals who have been fooled by the 'switch', whereby someone knocks on the door and tells them that they need money quickly because they need to get back to wherever they come from to their poorly wife and child. All they have is a couple of gold bars and coins etc. and because they are so desperate they will sell them to you at a very advantageous price.

Individuals have been known to accompany the scammer to a jeweller who tests the gold bars and coins and confirms that they are in fact real. He values them and the scammer accompanies the prospective investor to the bank to withdraw cash.

During this process, the briefcase or container with the gold bars and coins is switched. Unsurprisingly it contains no more than brass bars or a piece of lead.

In the last 12 months, I have known a local jeweller who was fooled by this scam.

If you're going to invest in paper gold, do beware of fictitious mining companies with a prospectus indicating a massive potential gold find. There are often surveyors' reports, chemists' reports as well as tall tales of previous successes. Over the years many investors have lost millions of dollars in these paper companies with absolutely no gold reserves.

Gold vs Equities

There are literally thousands of so-called investment 'instruments'. Bonds, bank deposits, mortgages, money market funds etc. There was a time when many of us thought that these types of investments were safe. Unfortunately, history has taught us that *every* investment has a risk attached to it. Nowadays, the same even applies to precious metals.

One of the world's great investment gurus Warren Buffett has pointed out that since 1965, the total return on gold was 4.455%, whereas the return on equities has been 6.072%.

So you can see that gold has not only underperformed stocks by 25% but the more interesting thing is that it has done so without tarnishing its image.

Buffett goes on to say that at most times, an investor is far better off investing in stocks rather than gold unless the monetary system is in danger, when gold becomes the favoured investment.

It all depends on what you want and what you are looking for as an investor. As I've already pointed out gold will not give you an income and historically, the upside associated with equities is far greater – as is the risk.

Currently, the global economy is still in the middle of what can best be termed as the 'great correction' and for the next few years it does seem that there is no particular reason why gold should rise unless of course there is another global financial crisis. Many economists believe that the global economy will continue to plod along in its current state of moribund chaos for the foreseeable future – but you never know!

If you are a pessimist and tightly focused on the rather fragile condition of the global political world and you see the amazing levels of debt that Western economies are carrying – and they are adding massive amounts daily to their burden – and you are aware of the huge array of companies which are no more than zombie organisations, you cannot fail to consider gold as an investment – because the overall prognosis is not the best.

If however, in spite of the fact that most working people have not had a proper increase in wages for several years and that our ancient democracies appear to be ailing with both national and personal debts reaching record levels and yet you still feel optimistic, then you should be thinking about investing in equities.

The real truth is that you should be aiming for somewhere in between with gold representing let's say 10% of your overall investment but always remember the rule that you should sell equities during rallies and buy gold during dips.

That way you will enjoy the best of both worlds!

Government Attitudes to Gold

There was a time when gold was not only an expression of wealth for the private individual but for whole countries. Sadly, that is no longer the case.

It would seem that gold is gradually turning from being no more than a very precious metal to becoming a commodity although at the present time we are in the transitional phase.

In the United Kingdom, as recently as 1966 private individuals were banned from owning more than four gold coins and only being able to buy them if they were granted a licence.

The incompetent mismanagement of economies by politicians can lead to all sorts of anomalies and unusual acts and we should do well to remember that it is not beyond the realms of possibility for any government finding itself in trouble to confiscate not only bank deposits but gold.

If you don't believe that is possible, think about the most sacrosanct of all investments that a private individual can hold – his or her pension. Hungary and Argentina have both nationalised private pension schemes.

All that government has to do in order to raid pensions is to change the tax regime and help itself. The same applies to commodities and that includes gold.

Having said all that the doomsday scenario I just described above is very unlikely to happen especially because of the latest fashion for central banks to print money when they sense trouble looming.

Just to put your mind at ease, even if governments confiscated our privately held gold, the value of it would barely be one .5% of total global economic output... so it's not really worth doing.

The link between gold and currencies has now been totally broken and that is why we no longer hear the term Gold Standard. Since the gradual decline of the gold standard, the amount of money sloshing about in the world is much higher than the total of the world's gold stocks.

Nevertheless, the demand for gold has fallen in recent years as it is no longer regarded as strong a hedge against risk as it used to be but interestingly, central banks are now beginning to buy gold.

Conclusion

In spite of all the negatives, gold's future as a viable investment remains intact. It has taken a battering in recent years but this appeal as a safe haven although shaken and stirred has remained intact. Every serious investor has gold within his or her portfolio.

Incredibly low interest rates added to the spectre of continued currency devaluations makes gold an excellent alternative plus the fact that if there are governments which are looking for additional income as a result of economic mismanagement, they are far more likely to tax equities and bonds rather than gold.

Gold has not fallen out of favour. All that has happened is that there are many more investments available to the private individual – property is such an investment which has only come to the fore in recent years – and it has most of the investment qualities of the precious metal.

I would therefore urge you to consider dipping your toe in the water with a small gold investment but if you are a long-term serious investor, do make sure that you don't put all of your eggs in one basket and invest in a whole range of products with your gold ever present as a hedge against the rest of your portfolio.